or the love of **CARMEL, MONTEREY,** and **PACIFIC GROVE**

Jim Brick

Jennie Brick

SCENIC NATURAL COOKBOOK

Photographs by Jim Brick

Recipes by Jennie Brick

All photographs in this book are available as stock photographs and display prints. Contact Visual Impressions directly.

Visual Impressions Publishing
820 Sweetbay Drive
Sunnyvale, CA 94086, USA
tel: 408-296-1629
fax: 408-244-3172

All photographs were taken with a Leica-R camera, Leica lenses from 24mm through 350mm, and the Leica 2x extender. Films used were Fujichrome 50 & 100 professional , and Kodachrome 200.

Jim Brick received his photographic education at Brooks Institute of Photography in Santa Barbara, California.

5-00-X
Printed in Hong Kong by Everbest Printing Co. Ltd.

9 8 7 6 5 4 3 2

Introduction

This book came about because of our love for the Carmel, Monterey, Pacific Grove area. The scenic beauty is unsurpassed. Each of the towns, the county, and the state, do a terrific job in maintaining the delicate balance between providing scenic access for tourists and keeping the ecology unharmed. The pictures in this book are proof that the scenic beauty can be enjoyed and photographed without invading the ecology.

Typically scenic books of tourist areas are simply that, scenic picture books. Buy it. Look at it. Put it on the bookshelf and forget it. Could a scenic book also be a useful book? We think so. How about a cookbook... Cookbooks are very useful. Everyone likes to try new recipes. You keep cookbooks handy because there is at least one recipe in every cookbook that you really like. If that recipe you want happens to be in a scenic cookbook, think of the memories brought back when you look at the pictures. The book won't be lost on a forgotten bookshelf. It will be nearby whether you want to look at the pictures or prepare one of the recipes.

The reason this is a <u>natural cookbook</u> is because this is how our family eats. We are raising four healthy children on the low fat, low cholestrol, high fiber philosophy depicted by these recipes. And, of course, these recipes are our family's favorites.

This cookbook is a companion of "for the love of CARMEL, MONTEREY, and PACIF GROVE, a SCENIC ADDRESS BOOK". The address book contains thirty beautiful scenic views Carmel, Monterey, and Pacific Grove alternating with address book pages, note pages, and specia pages.

Jim & Je

Vegetarian Vegetable Soup

7 cups water
1 cup small white beans
1 carrot, chopped
1 potato, diced
1 celery stalk, chopped
¾ cup green beans, cut in 1" lengths
½ tsp marjoram
½ tsp thyme
½ tsp basil
2 cups chopped tomatoes and liquid
½ tsp salt
⅛ tsp pepper
¾ cup peas, fresh or frozen
¾ cup corn, fresh or frozen

Cook white beans in water 45 minutes to 1 hour (until almost tender).
Add carrots, potatoes, celery, green beans, marjoram, thyme, basil,
tomatoes and their liquid, salt, and pepper. Simmer 20-30 minutes until
vegetables are tender. Add corn and peas and simmer for 5 minutes.

The Lone Cypress at dusk.

Fabulous Fish

YIELD: 4 servings

1 lb. of firm white fish filets
1 tbs soy sauce
1 tbs peanut oil
1 garlic clove, minced
¼ tsp ground ginger

Mix all ingredients, except fish, in a flat dish. Put fish into
mixture and turn to coat. Refrigerate for at least 1 hour.

Place fish on broiler pan. Broil about 8 minutes or until fish
flakes easily when tested with a fork.

A Harbor Seal mom and her pup near Cypress Point on 17 Mile Drive.

Tofu Mexicano

1 tbs olive or peanut oil
1 small onion, chopped
1 lb. firm tofu, well drained and mashed
4 oz. can diced green chilis
4 oz. can chopped olives
8 oz. can tomato sauce

Saute the onion in oil until softened. Add the remaining ingredients and bring to a boil. Simmer, uncovered, for 20 minutes.

Makes enough filling for 12 tacos or enchiladas.

This recipe makes a great filling for tacos and enchiladas.

Carmel Mission, built in 1770 under the direction of Father Junipero Serra.

Carrot Cake

3 cups grated carrots
2 cups honey
1 cup olive oil
1 cup water
3 tsp nutmeg
5 tsp cinnamon
2 cups raisins
⅔ cup nonfat or soy milk
3 egg whites
4 cups whole wheat pastry flour
2 tbs baking powder.

BAKE: 325º
TIME: 45-50 minutes
YIELD: 18 pieces

In a 5 quart saucepan, combine carrots, honey, oil, water, nutmeg, cinnamon, and raisins. Bring to a boil, simmer for 5 minutes. Cool. Beat egg whites slightly. Add to cooled carrot mixture along with milk. Stir flour and baking powder together. Add to mixture. Mix until blended. Bake in a greased and floured 9 x 13 x 2 inch pan.

For special occasions, frost with 6 oz. cream cheese whipped with 3 tbs honey

Looking toward Spanish Bay from Asilomar State Beach.

Graham Crackers

2 cups whole wheat flour
¼ tsp salt
1 tsp baking powder
½ tsp baking soda
1 tsp cinnamon
¼ cup olive oil
3 tbs honey
2 tbs molasses

BAKE: 300°
TIME: 20 minutes

Combine dry ingredients in a mixing bowl. Combine liquid ingredients in another bowl. Stir liquid mixture into dry mixture. Mix until smooth. Knead with hands to form a ball. If mixture is too dry, add water. If mixture is too wet, add flour.

Roll dough, ½ at a time, on a lightly floured surface, into a rectangle ⅛" thick. Prick dough evenly all over with a fork. Cut into 2" squares. Place ½" apart on lightly oiled cookie sheet.

Bake until firm and lightly browned. Cool on a rack.

Monastery Beach, a favorite place for scuba divers.

Oriental Shrimp Soup

1 tbs sesame or peanut oil
1 large onion, chopped
3 stalks celery, sliced ½" thick
2 carrots, sliced ¼" thick
2 cups sliced mushrooms
9 cups water
3 tsp ginger juice (see note)
1½ cups snow peas
2 cans sliced water chestnuts
6 tbs tamari
2 cups fresh mung bean sprouts
3 cups coarsley chopped fresh spinach
1 lb. cooked shrimp

In a 6 or 8 quart pot, heat oil. Add onion, celery, carrots, and mushrooms. Saute, stirring often, until vegetables are slightly tender. Add water and ginger juice. Bring to a boil. Reduce heat to simmer and cook for 10 minutes. Add snow peas and water chestnuts. Simmer for 5 minutes. Add tamari, bean sprouts, spinach, and shrimp. Heat until the spinach just wilts. Serve immediately.

Note: Grate 4" long piece of ginger root. Squeeze grated ginger in your hand letting the juice run into a cup.

Fisherman's Wharf in Monterey.

Apple Cake

½ cup oil
½ cup honey
3 egg whites
½ cup nonfat or soy milk
2 ½ cups whole wheat pastry flour
3 tsp baking powder
3 large apples, pared and sliced
⅓ cup honey
1 tsp mace
1 tsp grated lemon rind
1 tsp oil

BAKE: 350⁰
TIME: 30-40 minutes
YIELD: 12 pieces

Mix the ½ cup oil and the ½ cup honey together. Add egg whites and beat until creamy. Add milk and mix. Mix flour and baking powder together. Add to the honey mixture and stir until well blended. Pour into greased 9 x 13 x 2 inch pan. Arrange apples, overlapping slightly, in three lengthwise rows to cover top.

Combine ⅓ cup honey, mace, lemon rind, and oil, heat slightly. Pour over apples. Bake until a wooden pick, inserted in the center, comes out clean. Cut in squares and serve warm or cold.

Try with other fruits in place of apples. We like cherries or apricots.

The Seven Gables Inn overlooks Monterey Bay in Pacific Grove.

Honey-Carob Brownies

2 cups whole wheat flour
2 tsp baking powder
½ tsp salt
½ tsp cinnamon
1 cup olive oil
1 cup carob powder
1 cup honey
3 egg whites
1 cup broken walnuts (optional)
2 tsp vanilla extract
¼ cup nonfat or soy milk

BAKE: 350°
TIME: 20-25 minutes
YIELD: 12 squares

Stir together flour, baking powder, salt, and cinnamon. Set aside. Beat egg whites slightly in mixer bowl. Add honey, oil, and carob. Beat until smooth. Add flour mixture and blend. Add milk, vanilla, and nuts. Pour into a greased 9 x 13 x 2 inch pan and bake until firm, but not dry.

Cut into 12 square brownies.

Lovers looking at Lovers Point in Pacific Grove.

Jennie's Bread

6 cups water heated to 115° F
⅓ cup olive oil
⅓ cup honey
2 tbs salt
1 ½ cups gluten flour
2 tbs yeast
3 cups oat bran
14 cups (approximate) whole wheat flour

BAKE: 350°
TIME: 35 minutes
YIELD: 4 loaves

Put water, oil, honey, salt, gluten flour, and 5 cups of whole wheat flour in a large mixing bowl. Beat until smooth. Add yeast. Beat for 2 minutes. You can use an electric mixer until this point, but unless you have a mixer designed to knead bread, you will switch over to hand mixing. While mixing, add 3 cups of flour, one cup at a time. Add the oat bran in the same manner. Begin adding flour, a little at a time, until the dough is no longer sticky. Don't add so much that the dough gets dry. Put dough on a floured board and knead for at least 10 minutes. Place dough in a large oiled bowl. Turn dough over to grease top. Cover with a damp dish towel and let rise in a warm place (about 85° F) until dough size has doubled. Punch down. Cut dough into 4 equal pieces. Form each piece into a loaf and put in greased loaf pan. Cover with damp towel and let rise until dough size almost doubles. Bake until golden brown. Cool on racks.

Quaint shops, full of treasures, in downtown Carmel and the Crossroads.

Banana Nut Muffins

1 ¼ cups whole wheat pastry flour
2 tsp baking powder
¼ tsp baking soda
¼ tsp salt
½ cup chopped nuts
¼ cup honey
1 cup mashed ripe bananas
2 egg whites
1 tsp vanilla extract
⅓ cup olive oil

BAKE: 400°
TIME: 20 minutes
YIELD: 12 muffins

Combine dry ingredients in a bowl. Combine liquid ingredients in another bowl. Pour liquid ingredients into dry ingredients and stir until just moist. **Do not overbeat the muffin batter.** Overbeating will cause the gluten in the wheat flour to over develop and toughen the texture.

Fill greased muffin tins ¾ full and bake.

Adapted from the Cobblestone Inn recipe.

The Cobblestone Inn and innkeepers - our favorite.

Baked Beans

BAKE: 350°
TIME: 45 minutes
YIELD: 4-6 servings

6 cups cooked small white beans
1 ¼ cup liquid from cooking beans
2 tbs olive oil
1 onion, chopped
¼ cup tomato paste
¼ cup unsulphured molasses
1 ½ tsp dry mustard
1 tsp salt

Preheat oven to 350°. Saute' onion in oil until softened.
Add bean cooking liquid, tomato paste, molasses, mustard,
and salt. Mix well. Place beans in a 2 quart casserole.
Pour mixture over beans and mix. Cover and bake.

*Goes great with the
Brown Bread on the
next page.*

Fisherman's Shoreline Park in Monterey

Brown Bread

2 cups nonfat milk
2 tbs apple cider vinegar
¼ cup blackstrap molasses
¼ cup honey
1 ¼ cups raisins
1 cup whole wheat pastry flour
1 cup rye flour
1 cup cornmeal
2 tsp baking soda
1 tsp salt

In medium bowl, combine milk and vinegar. Let stand 10 minutes to
"sour". Add molasses, honey, and raisins. Combine dry ingredients in
another bowl. Mix wet and dry ingredients together. Pour mixture into
3 greased and floured cans (I use 20 oz. pineapple cans). Cover tightly
with foil. Tie securely with string. Place on rack in 5 quart saucepan.
Pour hot water into saucepan until it's halfway up side of cans. Bring to
a boil. Cover and boil 3 hours, adding more water to maintain level. If
bread won't slide out of can easily, use can opener to remove bottom
and push bread out.

YIELD: 3 loaves

*Goes great with the
Baked Beans on the
previous page.*

China Cove, Point Lobos State Reserve.

Scones

½ cup nonfat milk
1 ½ tsp cider vinegar
2 cups whole wheat pastry flour
½ tsp salt
¾ tsp soda
¼ cup oil
2 tbs honey
2 egg whites
½ cup currants or raisins

In a measuring cup or small bowl, mix milk and vinegar. Set aside for 10 minutes to "sour". In a mixing bowl, combine flour, salt, and soda. Beat egg whites until foamy. Add oil, honey, and sour milk. Add to flour mixture. Add raisins and mix. Place dough on floured board and knead about ½ minute. Pat or roll out ¾" thick. Cut into diamonds with a sharp knife or into rounds with a biscuit cutter. Place scones on ungreased baking sheet about 1" apart. Bake until light brown.

BAKE: 400°
TIME: 10 minutes
YIELD: 12 scones

These are great split and spread with "all fruit" preserves.

Quaint Carmel shops and Christmas at Carmel Plaza.

Gingerbread

BAKE: 350°
TIME: 25-30 minutes
YIELD: 12

¾ cup honey
¼ cup blackstrap molasses
¾ cup olive oil
3 egg whites
2½ cups whole wheat pastry flour
2½ tsp soda
½ tsp baking powder
1½ tsp ginger
½ tsp nutmeg
½ tsp cinnamon
1 cup boiling water
1 cup raisins

Beat honey, molasses, oil, and egg whites together. Stir flour, soda, baking powder, ginger, nutmeg, and cinnamon together. Add to honey mixture. Add water and raisins. Pour into a greased 9 x 13 x 2 inch pan and bake. Cut into 12 squares.

Colorful ice plant blooms along the Pacific Grove coastline.

Yummy Carrots

YIELD: 6 servings

5 medium size carrots, sliced ¼" thick
2 tbs honey
1 ½ tsp dijon mustard
1 tsp curry powder
1 ½ tsp lemon juice
½ cup raisins

Steam carrots about 10 minutes or until just tender. In a
10" skillet, mix honey, mustard, curry powder, and lemon
juice. Add carrots and raisins. Cook, stirring constantly, for
about 3 minutes, until the carrots are well glazed.

Giant Kelp Forest exhibit at the Monterey Bay Aquarium.

Favorite Tofu Casserole

1 tbs olive oil
1 medium onion, chopped
2 cloves garlic, minced
1 lb. firm tofu, well drained and mashed
1 28 oz. can crushed tomatoes
3 tbs chili powder
1½ tsp cumin
12 corn tortillas, cut into sixths
2 cups grated cheddar cheese
1 cup green onions, finely chopped
1 cup black olives, sliced

BAKE: 350°
TIME: 20 minutes
YIELD: 6-8 servings

Saute the onion and garlic in olive oil. When onion is soft, add tofu and cook for 2-3 minutes. Add tomatoes, chili powder, and cumin. Simmer for 25 minutes. Spread ¾ cup sauce in a 9 x 13 x 2 inch glass pan. Cover with half the tortilla pieces. Cover with ¾ of the sauce, then ¾ of the cheese, olives, and green onions. Repeat layers starting with remaining tortilla pieces. Bake for 20 minutes.

Even better the next day!

Orphaned sea otters feeding and learning, Sea Anemones, and children at the Touch Pool are all part of the daily routine at the Monterey Bay Aquarium.

Make Your Own Tuna Salad

YIELD: serves 6

8 cups of your favorite salad greens
1½ cups cucumber slices
2 20 oz. cans pineapple chunks, drained (save juice)
1 cup sliced green onions
3 6 oz. cans solid white tuna in water, drained and broken
    into chunks
2 carrots, grated
1½ cups shredded red cabbage

DRESSING

6 tbs pineapple juice
1 tsp dill weed
1 cup mayonnaise
1 tsp Spike, or other seasoned salt

Serve the greens in a salad bowl. Serve the other ingredients in
separate bowls. Each person puts a bed of greens on his plate, then
adds the ingredients he likes. Then please pass the dressing.

*Keep tuna and
pineapple in fridge,
all ready to serve on
a "too hot to cook"
summer day.*

*Serve with whole wheat
crackers.*

The Tide Pool at the Monterey Bay Aquarium is open to Monterey Bay.

Rice With Shrimp and Scallops

YIELD: 6 servings

2 cups uncooked long-grain brown rice
2 tbs olive or peanut oil
1 large onion, chopped
4 fresh tomatoes, chopped
3 cups vegetable stock
¾ lb. shrimp
¾ lb. scallops
½ cup chopped parsley
⅛ tsp pepper

Saute rice in oil until lightly browned. Add onion. Saute 3-5 minutes.
Add tomatoes and vegetable stock. Cover and cook 35 minutes over low
heat. Add shrimp and scallops. Cook 15 minutes or until rice is done. Stir
in parsley and pepper.

Fish market on Fisherman's Wharf, Monterey.

Twice-Baked Potatoes

6 medium brown potatoes
olive oil
2 medium carrots
1 bunch broccoli
¼ cup nonfat milk
1 tsp salt
⅛ tsp pepper
½ cup grated cheese

BAKE: 400°
TIME: 60-75 minutes
YIELD: serves 6

Preheat oven to 400° F. Scrub and dry potatoes. Rub olive oil into potato skins. Bake potatoes 45-60 minutes until done. Peel and slice carrots. Peel broccoli stems. Steam broccoli and carrots until just done. Finely chop broccoli and carrots. When potatoes are cool enough to handle, cut them in half lengthwise. Scoop out inside of potatoes and mash well. Add broccoli, carrots, milk, salt, and pepper. Mash until evenly mixed. Spoon potato mixture into skins and place on baking sheet. Sprinkle with cheese. Place in oven for 10-15 minutes until hot and the cheese is melted.

Sunset at Carmel beach.

Clam Chowder

YIELD: 4-6 servings

2   *tbs olive oil*
½   *cup minced onion*
2   *7 oz. cans minced or whole clams*
2   *cups finely diced raw potatoes*
½   *cup water*
2   *cups nonfat milk*
⅛   *tsp pepper*

In 4 quart saucepan, saute onion in olive oil. Add liquid from clams, water, and potatoes. Cook about 10 minutes until potatoes are tender. Add milk, pepper, and clams. Heat to just boiling, stirring occasionally. Serve.

Hobie Cat races in Monterey Bay.

Vegetarian Chili

YIELD: serves 6-8

3 cups dried pinto beans
8 cups water
4 cloves garlic, minced
¾ tsp cumin
2 onions, chopped
2 tbs olive oil
2 15 oz. cans tomato sauce
2 cups corn, fresh or frozen
2 tbs chili powder

Wash and sort through beans, discarding rocks and imperfect beans.
Cook beans in water with garlic and cumin until almost tender.
Meanwhile saute onion in olive oil until golden. Add onions to the
cooked beans along with the rest of the ingredients. Simmer for 30
minutes, or more, until beans are tender.

A Monarch Butterfly in Butterfly Town, USA (Pacific Grove).

Orange-Onion Salad

YIELD: serves 6

2 *naval oranges, peeled and sliced crosswise*
1 *red onion, sliced into thin rings*
lettuce - fill a serving bowl with your favorites

<u>*DRESSING*</u>

¾ *cup olive oil*
¼ *cup lemon juice*
½ *tsp salt*
½ *tsp lemon rind*
¼ *tsp dry mustard*

Place all ingredients in a jar and shake well. Spoon some dressing over salad greens, orange, and onion rings. Toss to coat.

Monarch Butterflies hang in clusters in the Monterey Pines of Washington Park, Pacific Grove.

Artichokes

TIME: 40-60 minutes
YIELD: serves 6

6 *medium or large artichokes*
3 *cloves garlic, cut in half lengthwise*
1 *tbs olive oil*
6 *thin slices of lemon*

Choose a pan which will fit all of the artichokes sitting upright. Put about 1" of water in pan. Add garlic, oil, and lemon to water. Bring to a boil.

Trim artichoke stem to within ¼" of base. With scissors, cut about ½" off each leaf point. Use a sharp knife, or bread knife, to cut off top 1" of artichoke. Wash artichokes well. Place artichokes stem side down in boiling water. Lower heat to simmer, cover pan. Cook 40-60 minutes, depending on size of artichokes. To test for doneness, pull out a leaf, located about half way between outside and center. The leaf base should be tender.

Near Point Joe, on 17 Mile Drive, surfers wait for the next wave as Pelicans cruise by.

Terrific Tomato Soup

¼ cup olive oil
6 tbs whole wheat pastry flour
1 tsp curry powder
pinch of pepper
2 15 oz. cans tomato sauce
4 cups nonfat milk

Heat oil in a 3 quart saucepan. Add flour and curry powder. Cook for a full minute. Slowly add tomato sauce while stirring constantly. Add pepper. Bring mixture to a boil, while stirring. Add milk. Heat until warm enough to serve, stirring occasionally.

Variation: Omit curry powder, substitute 1 tsp dried basil.

Looking south along the Pacific coastline from Cypress Point on 17 Mile Drive.

Gingersnaps

¾ cup olive oil
¼ cup blackstrap molasses
⅔ cup honey
3 cups whole wheat pastry flour
¼ cup wheat germ
1½ tsp soda
½ tsp cream of tartar
3 tsp ground ginger
1 tsp cinnamon
¼ tsp allspice

BAKE: 350⁰
TIME: 7-9 minutes
YIELD: 5 dozen

Mix liquid ingredients in a bowl. In a separate bowl, combine dry ingredients. Stir liquid ingredients into dry ingredients until well blended. Roll cookie dough into balls about the size of a small walnut. Place on cookie sheet and flatten to about ⅛" thick with the bottom of a glass that has been dipped in flour. Bake until slightly browned. Cool on racks.

Flowers in a Carmel alleyway and the La Playa Hotel gardens.

Peanut Butter Banana Cookies

1 cup peanut butter
½ cup peanut oil
1¼ cups honey
1 cup mashed bananas (2 medium bananas)
2 tsp vanilla
3 cups whole wheat pastry flour
2 tsp soda
1 tsp baking powder
1 tsp cinnamon
½ tsp nutmeg

BAKE: 350°
TIME: 12 minutes
YIELD: 5 dozen

Cream together peanut butter, oil, and honey. Add bananas and vanilla. Stir dry ingredients together, then into creamed mixture until well blended. Drop teaspoonfuls of dough onto oiled cookie sheet and bake.

The Barnyard Shopping Center. Shop and dine in a country garden setting.

Pleasing Potato Soup

YIELD: serves 6

1 onion, chopped
1 clove garlic, minced
1 tbs olive oil
2 cups water
5 medium russet potatoes, peeled and cut into ½" cubes
2 large red potatoes, unpeeled, cut into ½" cubes
½ cup water
3 cups nonfat or soy milk
1 tsp salt
¼ tsp pepper
1 cup grated sharp cheddar cheese
2 tbs chopped parsley

In 5 quart pan, saute onion and garlic in oil, until soft. Add 2 cups water and russet potatoes. Cook 10-15 minutes or until potatoes are soft. Meanwhile, in a small pan, cook red potatoes in ½ cup water until just tender. Put onion-potato mixture through blender and put back in pan. Stir in milk, salt, pepper, cheese, parsley, and red potatoes with cooking water. Heat until very hot, but do not boil.

So good on a cold winter night with a green salad and dark rye bread.

Even better the nexy day.

Miles and miles of golf courses follow the coastline on 17 Mile Drive.

Tuna and Noodles

3 tbs olive oil
3 cups sliced mushrooms
¼ cup minced onions
5 cups vegetable broth
12 oz. uncooked whole wheat spagetti, broken into 3" lengths
4 tbs whole wheat flour
1½ cups nonfat milk
5 tbs sherry
¼ tsp pepper
⅛ tsp nutmeg
3 6 oz. cans tuna, drained
3 tbs chopped parsley

YIELD: serves 6-8

Saute mushrooms and onions in 1 tbs oil, then set aside. Bring vegetable broth to a boil in a 12" fry pan with lid. Add spagetti, cover and simmer for 15-18 minutes until cooked. Do not drain. Meanwhile, heat 2 tbs oil in 1 quart saucepan, add flour, cook for 1 minute. Stir in slowly; milk, sherry, pepper, and nutmeg. Cook, stirring constantly, until almost boiling. Add to cooked spagetti, mix well. Add tuna, heat through. Sprinkle parsley over top.

Two local attractions; Clint Eastwood's place and Hero, the parrot, talking to passers-by at Vendetti's.

Cabbage-Apple Salad

3 cups shredded green cabbage
1 cup shredded red cabbage
3 cups diced red apples
½ cup thinly sliced celery
½ cup raisins
½ cup mayonnaise
3 tbs lemon juice
1 tsp salt
pepper to taste

Combine all ingredients in a large bowl. Chill well.

Sunset over Point Lobos from Monastery Beach.

Carrot-Bran Muffins

1 ½ cups whole wheat pastry flour
¾ cup wheat bran
¾ cup oat bran
2 tsp baking soda
2 tsp cinnamon
¾ tsp nutmeg
½ tsp ginger
½ cup raisins
3 egg whites
1 ½ cups nonfat milk
2 tbs cider vinegar
¼ cup olive oil
¾ cup honey
1 cup grated carrot
½ cup chopped nuts

BAKE: 375º
TIME: 20 minutes
YIELD: 24

Stir dry ingredients and raisins together. Combine egg whites, milk, vinegar, oil, and honey. Add liquid ingredients to dry ingredients and stir just until moistened. Add carrots and nuts. Fill greased muffin tins ¾ full.

Adapted from the Cobblestone Inn recipe.

Storm clouds over Monterey harbor.

A few helpful hints...

Use a mixture of ½ liquid lecithin and ½ peanut oil to grease baking pans. Use a pastry brush to apply. This is a healthier alternative to solid shortening or butter.

When measuring oil and honey for a recipe, measure the oil first. This will coat the measuring jug and the honey will slip right out.

All unfamiliar sounding ingredients should be available at your local health food store.

...Jennie Brick